KU-620-031

SPOTLIGHTS

THE EGYPTIANS

Written by Neil Grant

ANDROMEDA

ACKNOWLEDGMENTS

Illustrated by
Richard Berridge
Philip Hood
Richard Hook
Bill Le Fever
The Maltings Partnership
Tony Smith
Clive Spong

Picture credits
Front Cover Andromeda; **Back Cover**
Andromeda, Michael Holford

Devised and produced by
Andromeda Oxford Limited
11-15 The Vineyard
Abingdon
Oxfordshire OX14 3PX

Copyright © 1993 Andromeda Oxford Limited
Reprinted 1996

All rights reserved. No part of this publication may be reproduced,
stored in a retrieval system or transmitted in any form or by any
means electronic, mechanical, photocopying, recording or otherwise,
without the permission of the copyright holders.

ISBN 1 871869 92 7
Printed in Singapore by Tien Wah Press

CONTENTS

INTRODUCTION 6

EGYPT AND THE NILE 8

THE OLD KINGDOM 10

BUILDING THE PYRAMIDS 12

THE MIDDLE KINGDOM 14

PHARAOHS 16

THE NEW KINGDOM 18

RELIGION 20

PREPARING FOR THE NEXT WORLD 22

TOWNS AND CITIES 24

SCULPTURE AND PAINTING 26

CRAFTSMEN 28

WRITING 30

CHILDREN AND EDUCATION 32

FARMERS 34

TRADE AND SHIPS 36

FAMILY LIFE 38

FOOD AND DRINK 40

GAMES AND HUNTING 42

GLOSSARY 44

INDEX 46

INTRODUCTION

Over 5,000 years ago, the world's first civilized nation was born on the banks of the River Nile, in Egypt. It was not the only centre of civilization, large cities already existed not far away, in Mesopotamia (modern Iraq). But the people of Mesopotamia were not a nation. Each city had a different king, different laws and different gods. Egyptians were ruled by one king, obeyed the same laws, and worshipped the same gods.

The civilization of ancient Egypt lasted for about 3,000 years. That is much longer than our own civilization has lasted. For that reason at least, the world's first civilization was also one of the most successful.

VISITING MUSEUMS

The Egyptians made the tombs of their dead into museums of a kind, filling them with all kinds of objects as well as paintings and sculpture showing scenes of everyday life. Today, many of these objects can be seen in real museums all over the world. You can find nearly everything in this book in a museum with a good Egyptian collection.

HOW TO USE THIS BOOK

This book explores and explains the world of the ancient Eygptians. Each double-page spread looks at a particular aspect of life in Eygpt, building up a fascinating picture of this important civilization.

INTRODUCTION

Concise yet highly informative, this text introduces the reader to the topics covered in the spread. This broad coverage is complemented by more detailed exploration of particular points in the numerous captions.

INSET ARTWORKS

Subjects that help to explain particular points are shown in inset along with an explanation of their significance.

SPOTLIGHTS

A series of illustrations at the bottom of each page encourages the reader to look out for objects from ancient Egypt that can be found in museums.

BUILDING

The biggest pyram seen at Giza, near the tombs of the ki Kingdom. The bigge Khufu or Cheops, a Dynasty. This pyram 100m high and conta million blocks of ston over 6 million tonnes. was brought by boats f quarries, and then drag site on sledges. Thousan people worked on the bu which took about 23 yea complete.

INSIDE THE PYRAMID

The burial chamber itself was deep inside the pyramid. Other rooms held objects the king might need in the next life. After the burial, workmen slid stone blocks down the passages to try to keep out thieves.

cap sto

burial chamber

LOOK OUT FOR THESE

STONEMASO TOOLS
In the quarry, large chunks of stone wer broken off by pushi wooden wedges into cracks. Blocks were then shaped with a chisel and mallet.

12

HEADING
The subject matter of each spread is clearly identified by a heading prominently displayed in the top left-hand corner.

DETAILED INFORMATION
From the building of their extraordinary pyramids and temples to the everyday life of Egyptian families, the reader is given a wealth of information to help understand the ancient Eygptians.

ILLUSTRATIONS
High quality, full colour artworks bring the world of the Egyptians to life. Each spread is packed with visual information.

REFERENCE TAB
Each group of subjects is keyed with a special colour to the contents page of the book so that different sections can be found quickly and easily.

YRAMIDS

RAISING STONE BLOCKS
One of the hardest jobs was moving the heavy stone blocks into place. The builders made huge ramps of earth, and dragged the stones up the ramps with ropes.

air passages

entrance

SUPERVISORS
Officials, who were probably priests, directed the gangs of workmen.

SHAPING THE STONE
Each stone was carefully measured and shaped to fit into place.

ACCIDENTS
Many workmen were killed or injured, crushed by the heavy stone blocks.

s and
e were
den
had to be
a
es this.

STEP PYRAMID
The first pyramids did not have smooth sides. They were left in the form of platforms or steps. Step pyramids were also built by other ancient peoples.

LEATHER BAG
Thousands of men worked on each pyramid, and they all needed food and drink. Water was often carried in leather bags made from animal skins.

CHECKING MEASUREMENTS
Stonemasons used right-angles and plumb lines to make sure the side of the stone blocks were straight. Such tools are still used today.

EGYPT AND THE NILE

Ancient Egypt was a strange shape. It looked like a flower on a long stem. The stem was the valley of the River Nile, and the flower was the Delta. People's lives depended on the Nile. Everyone lived in a strip of green land along the river.

Egypt is a dry land. Without the Nile, it would be all desert. The Nile was also the main highway, joining cities hundreds of kilometres apart.

Every September, the Nile overflowed and left a layer of black silt, which was so rich that the farmers could grow two or three crops a year.

Mediterranean Sea · Delta · LOWER EGYPT · Memphis · Faiyum Lake

THE DELTA
North of Memphis, the Nile divided into channels, to form a delta. Much of this land was swampy, but the rest was good for farming.

OASIS
The Western Desert had a few places where enough water was available for crops to be grown.

LOOK OUT FOR THESE

ANIMAL GOD
The Egyptians believed that gods and goddesses could appear as human beings or as animals (or as humans with animal heads). Anubis, a god of the dead, was a dog or jackal.

NEFERTITI
This is a famous Egyptian work of art. It is the head of Nefertiti, a queen of the 18th Dynasty, and it is made of stone, covered with plaster and painted. The head is now in a museum in Berlin, in Germany. It has become a symbol of Ancient Egypt.

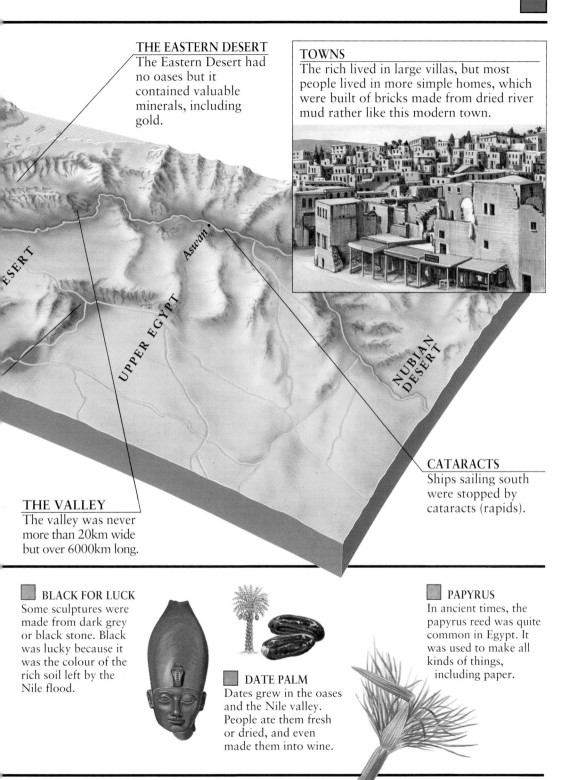

THE EASTERN DESERT
The Eastern Desert had no oases but it contained valuable minerals, including gold.

TOWNS
The rich lived in large villas, but most people lived in more simple homes, which were built of bricks made from dried river mud rather like this modern town.

ESERT

Aswan

UPPER EGYPT

NUBIAN DESERT

CATARACTS
Ships sailing south were stopped by cataracts (rapids).

THE VALLEY
The valley was never more than 20km wide but over 6000km long.

BLACK FOR LUCK
Some sculptures were made from dark grey or black stone. Black was lucky because it was the colour of the rich soil left by the Nile flood.

DATE PALM
Dates grew in the oases and the Nile valley. People ate them fresh or dried, and even made them into wine.

PAPYRUS
In ancient times, the papyrus reed was quite common in Egypt. It was used to make all kinds of things, including paper.

THE OLD KINGDOM

Upper Egypt (the Nile valley) and Lower Egypt (the Delta) were united as one country over 5,000 years ago.

By the 3rd Dynasty, the kingdom was rich and powerful. Its kings, or pharaohs, were believed to be living gods. When they died, they were buried in huge tombs, called pyramids, and their bodies were often carried to the burial place by special funeral boats.

By the 5th Dynasty, the kingdom was breaking down. Kings lost their power. The Nile flood failed for several years, causing famine. The country became divided again, until the 11th Dynasty.

ROYAL FUNERAL
The pharaoh's body was brought by boat to a valley temple. From there, it was carried into the pyramid.

FUNERAL BOAT
A special boat was built for the pharaoh. Later the boat itself was buried near the tomb.

LOOK OUT FOR THESE

SPHINX
A sphinx has a human head and a lion's body. A huge stone sphinx guards the pyramids of Giza, but there were many others, large and small.

NAME PLATE
In the picture-writing of ancient Egypt, the name of a ruler is written inside an oval.

COFFIN

The body was 'mummified' to preserve it, then placed in several coffins.

TIMETABLE

The civilization of Ancient Egypt lasted nearly 3,000 years. It was divided into kingdoms and dynasties (ruling families). During the Intermediate Periods, Egypt was not united.

Early Period 3100–2600 BC
1st–3rd Dynasties

OLD KINGDOM 2600–2134 BC
4th–7th Dynasties

First Intermediate Period
2134–2040 BC

MIDDLE KINGDOM
2040–1640 BC
11th–14th Dynasties

Second Intermediate Period
1640–1550 BC

NEW KINGDOM
1550–1070 BC
18th–20th Dynasties

Third Intermediate Period
1070–712 BC

Late Period 712–332 BC

MEMORIAL

Some early kings of Egypt ordered records of their deeds to be carved on stone slabs. This is the Palette of King Narmer. He was probably the first ruler of a united Egypt and the palette records his victories in battle.

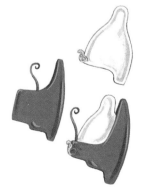

ROYAL CROWNS

Pictures of kings show them wearing the White Crown of Upper Egypt, or the Red Crown of Lower Egypt. Sometimes, they wear a combined crown, as a sign that they ruled the whole country.

BUILDING THE PYRAMIDS

The biggest pyramids can still be seen at Giza, near Cairo. They are the tombs of the kings of the Old Kingdom. The biggest belonged to Khufu or Cheops, a king of the 4th Dynasty. This pyramid is over 100m high and contains 2.3 million blocks of stone, weighing over 6 million tonnes. The stone was brought by boats from the quarries, and then dragged to the site on sledges. Thousands of people worked on the building, which took about 23 years to complete.

RAISING STONE BLOCKS

One of the hardest jobs was moving the heavy stone blocks into place. The builders made huge ramps of earth, and dragged the stones up the ramps with ropes.

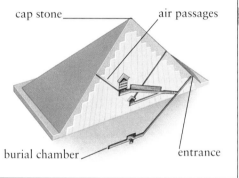

SUPERVISORS

Officials, who were probably priests, directed the gangs of workmen.

INSIDE THE PYRAMID

The burial chamber itself was deep inside the pyramid. Other rooms held objects the king might need in the next life. After the burial, workmen slid stone blocks down the passages to try to keep out thieves.

cap stone

air passages

burial chamber

entrance

LOOK OUT FOR THESE

STONEMASON'S TOOLS

In the quarry, large chunks of stone were broken off by pushing wooden wedges into cracks. Blocks were then shaped with a chisel and mallet.

ROLLERS

Heavy sledges and blocks of stone were moved on wooden rollers, which had to be kept damp. In a modern factory, a conveyor belt does this.

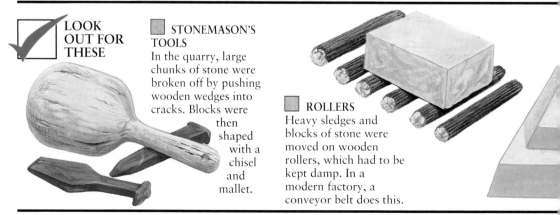

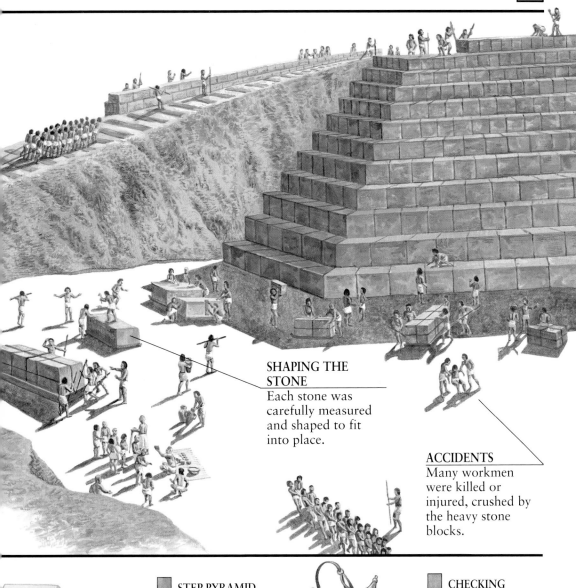

SHAPING THE STONE
Each stone was carefully measured and shaped to fit into place.

ACCIDENTS
Many workmen were killed or injured, crushed by the heavy stone blocks.

 STEP PYRAMID
The first pyramids did not have smooth sides. They were left in the form of platforms or steps. Step pyramids were also built by other ancient peoples.

 LEATHER BAG
Thousands of men worked on each pyramid, and they all needed food and drink. Water was often carried in leather bags made from animal skins.

 CHECKING MEASUREMENTS
Stonemasons used right-angles and plumb lines to make sure the side of the stone blocks were straight. Such tools are still used today.

THE MIDDLE KINGDOM

Egypt was united once more by the kings of the 11th Dynasty. Trade revived, and the country grew rich again. More farming land was gained by draining the Faiyum lake. New quarries and mines were dug in the Sinai Desert. Nubia was brought under Egyptian rule.

It was a great age of art and crafts. The language reached its finest form. Students of ancient Egypt today learn the language of the Middle Kingdom.

The kings of the 13th Dynasty were less powerful. Again, the royal government lost control. The kings of the 15th Dynasty were foreigners, known as the Hyskos.

DANCERS
Men did not dance much, but girl dancers performed at feasts. Dwarfs were popular jesters.

MUSICIANS
Musicians played many kinds of instruments, including reed pipes, harps, and a stringed instrument like a banjo.

☑ **LOOK OUT FOR THESE**

◻ **OBELISK**
These tall, square pillars were put up as monuments. The flat sides were covered with writing, and the top was pointed like a pyramid. Some have been taken to other countries.

◻ **'TOPKNOTS'**
Ladies wore cones like these on their heads in the evenings. They were made of scented wax and made their hair smell sweet.

◻ **MODEL BOAT**
Small models of useful objects, like this boat, were often placed in tombs, in case they were needed in the next life.

NUBIANS
People from Nubia, captured in war or sold into slavery, worked as servants.

MAIDSERVANTS
Rich people had many servants, mainly girls. At banquets, most of the entertainers and waitresses were young women.

FOOD AND DRINK
Rich people had a varied diet, with plenty of meat and vegetables. They drank wine or beer.

LOOM
Most clothes were made of linen. Women wove the thread into cloth on a loom, which was a simple, wooden frame. Threads running across (the weft) were woven in and out of the threads running up and down (the warp). Some Egyptian linen was so fine you could see through it.

A SCRIBE
Scribes, or writers, were clerks and managers. They kept records of trade, crops and animals, taxes, punishments and so on, for the government. Like all government officials, they were not very popular.

PHARAOHS

The king, or pharaoh, was not only the ruler of Egypt but he was also a god. In fact, he was several gods. As ruler, he was linked with the royal god Horus. Sometimes, he was seen as the sun god Ra. After his death, he became joined with Osiris, god of the dead.

Everything the god-king said or did was important. His life was a long series of ceremonies. The simplest act, such as washing his face, was performed as a religious act. Every little incident had a meaning. If the pharaoh had a headache, it meant bad luck for the whole kingdom.

ABU SIMBEL
The Great Temple of the sun god was built into the rock at Abu Simbel, in Nubia. At the entrance stood four huge statues of its builder, Ramesses II. In the 1960s, the whole building had to be moved to a higher place, above the level of the lake made by a new dam at Aswan.

TRIBUTE
Rulers of smaller countries recognized the king of Egypt as their overlord. They sent him tributes – expensive gifts – as a sign of loyalty.

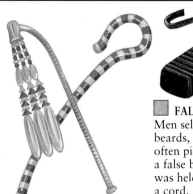

LOOK OUT FOR THESE

CROOK AND FLAIL
These were symbols of the god Osiris. They were also carried by the king at ceremonies. The crook became a ruler's symbol.

FALSE BEARD
Men seldom grew beards, but the king is often pictured wearing a false beard, which was held in place with a cord.

OSTRICH FAN
Fans made of ostrich feathers provided a cooling breeze in Egypt's hot climate.

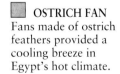

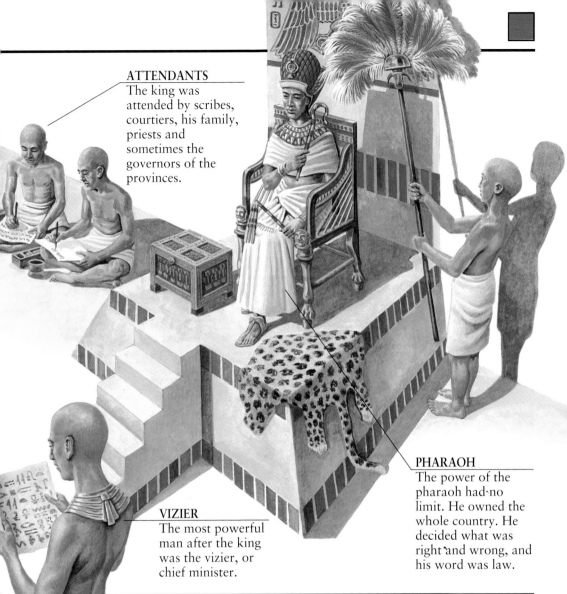

ATTENDANTS

The king was attended by scribes, courtiers, his family, priests and sometimes the governors of the provinces.

PHARAOH

The power of the pharaoh had·no limit. He owned the whole country. He decided what was right·and wrong, and his word was law.

VIZIER

The most powerful man after the king was the vizier, or chief minister.

■ ROYAL HEADDRESS

Kings often wore a headdress of striped linen, like this. Sometimes, they wore a crown on top. The objects on the forehead – a cobra and a vulture – were the king's protectors.

■ HORUS

The god Horus was often shown as a hawk. He was the god most closely linked with the living god-king. Here he is wearing the royal double-crown of Upper and Lower Egypt. It was believed that the spirit of the dead could take the form of a hawk.

THE NEW KINGDOM

The Hyskos were driven out by the kings of the New Kingdom. The kings also conquered an empire in the Middle East, whose people paid taxes to Egypt. But by the 19th Dynasty, Egypt itself was threatened by the warlike Hittites. Egypt's greatness began to fade, as rival dynasties fought for the throne.

Egypt could no longer defend itself. Foreign conquerors took over – first the Nubians, then the Assyrians and the Persians. The great days of Egypt were over.

PRISONERS OF WAR
Wars brought Egypt into closer contact with its neighbours. Prisoners were taken back to Egypt as slaves, or made to serve in the Egyptian army.

BATTLE
In the New Kingdom, Egyptian armies fought as far away as Mesopotamia (Iraq). They now had chariots, but their weapons were still mostly bronze. People like the Hittites had harder, iron weapons.

LOOK OUT FOR THESE

SPEAR
The royal guards carried swords. Foot soldiers carried a spear about 2m long. The point was bronze, and the shaft wooden.

DAGGER
Kings and officers wore daggers. This gold one is an ornament, which belonged to the pharaoh Tutankamun.

BATTLE AXE
For fighting at close quarters, a soldier had a battle axe. Some axes had curved blades, for slashing and slicing, but this type was used more like a club. The blade was copper.

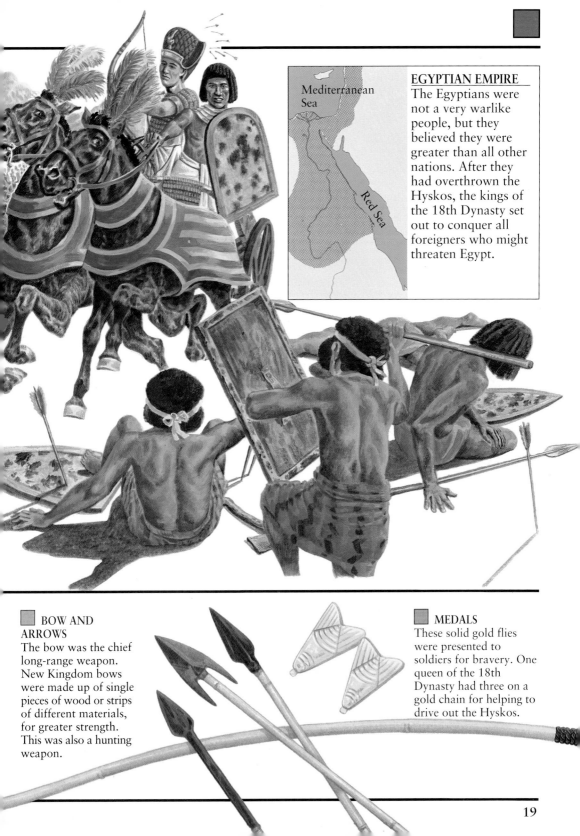

EGYPTIAN EMPIRE

The Egyptians were not a very warlike people, but they believed they were greater than all other nations. After they had overthrown the Hyskos, the kings of the 18th Dynasty set out to conquer all foreigners who might threaten Egypt.

Mediterranean Sea

Red Sea

BOW AND ARROWS

The bow was the chief long-range weapon. New Kingdom bows were made up of single pieces of wood or strips of different materials, for greater strength. This was also a hunting weapon.

MEDALS

These solid gold flies were presented to soldiers for bravery. One queen of the 18th Dynasty had three on a gold chain for helping to drive out the Hyskos.

RELIGION

The Egyptians worshipped hundreds of different gods and goddesses.

Religion was an important part of life, not something separate. Temples contained schools, workshops and storehouses, as well as being the home of the gods. Besides serving the gods, priests did many other jobs, such as teaching, or even helping with the harvest.

Religious festivals were holidays. The festival of the god Amun lasted for a month during the flood season, when no work had to be done in the fields.

HOME OF THE GOD
A temple was the palace or home of the god. Beyond the large hall was the sanctuary, containing the shrine of the god.

GODS AND GODDESSES
All the gods were related, but some were more important. Most gods had a sacred animal associated with them.

 LOOK OUT FOR THESE

WADJIT
Wadjit was a goddess of the Delta. She is shown with a lioness's head and a cobra on top. The cobra was a symbol of Lower Egypt.

OSIRIS
Osiris looked after the growth of plants, and had a green skin. He was both husband and brother of Isis. She restored him to life after he was killed by his evil brother, Seth, who seized the throne of Egypt. Osiris became king of the dead.

THE SHRINE
The god's statue stood in the sanctuary, which only the priests were allowed to enter.

PRIESTS
The priests had to be pure and clean. They shaved their heads and bodies and washed four times a day. They wore gowns of fine, white linen.

OFFERINGS
The chief priest brought daily offerings of food, and carried out other holy duties, such as washing and clothing the god.

STATUE
At religious festivals, priests carried the statue outside, where the people could pray to the god or ask him or her questions.

■ HATHOR
The goddess Hathor, who looked after women and children, wore a sun disc with cow's horns. Sometimes, she has a cow's head. She was the wife of Horus.

■ MAGIC EYE
The magic eye, or Eye of Horus, is a sign of the Sun or Moon. It was a good-luck sign and protected against evil spells.

■ ANKH
The Ankh was a sign meaning 'life'. It was carried only by gods and kings, who had power over life and death.

PREPARING FOR THE NEXT WORLD

The Egyptians believed that after a person died, he would live again in a kind of heaven. There he would need the same things that he needed in Egypt, including his body. When an important person died, priests performed many ceremonies to help the dead person on his journey to a happy life in the next world.

The priests of Anubis preserved the body by 'mummification'. This took about two months. The mummy was wrapped in strips of linen and placed inside a wooden coffin. That went into a stone coffin, which was carried to the tomb on a sledge. Afterwards, the burial chamber was blocked up.

The tomb was a 'home' for the dead. Every day, priests said prayers, provided food and guarded the dead man's household goods that were buried with him.

ANUBIS
The priest in charge of the mummification wore the mask of Anubis (the god of the dead).

NATRON
Natron, a kind of soda, was placed in the body to dry it out before it was wrapped in linen.

LOOK OUT FOR THESE

CANOPIC JARS
The insides of the body, including the brain, were placed in decorated jars. These were buried with the body.

MUMMIFIED HEAD
This mummified head of the pharaoh Seti I is over 3,000 years old. It is so well preserved that you can still see exactly what this powerful king looked like when he ruled Egypt.

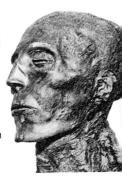

INCENSE

A priest stands by, holding sweet-smelling incense.

WRAPPING THE BODY

The body, or mummy, was wrapped in layers of linen before being placed in the coffin.

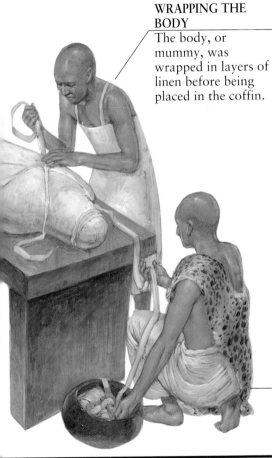

THE COFFIN

The wooden coffin was shaped to fit the body. It was beautifully painted, sometimes with a portrait of the dead person.

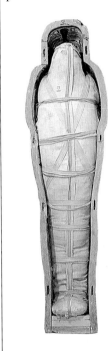

SOAKING THE BANDAGES

Sometimes, linen strips were soaked in plaster so they would harden when dry.

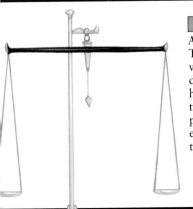

SCALES OF ANUBIS

The god Anubis weighed the dead person's heart on scales to see if the person was pure enough to enter the next life.

INCENSE JAR

Jars like this were used for burning scented gums, bark and flowers.

AMULETS

Magic charms, or amulets, were placed in the coffin to protect the mummy.

Towns and Cities

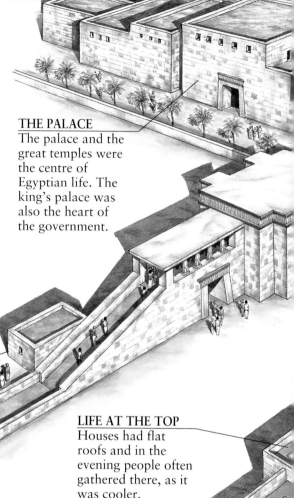

Egypt was a farming country, but it also had large cities, like Memphis, capital of the Old Kingdom. Cities often began as religious centres. Thebes, the greatest city of the New Kingdom, included the huge temples of Karnak and Luxor.

The ordinary people lived in plain, simple houses made of mud bricks, which looked very like houses in Egyptian villages today. They had high walls and small windows, without glass. Because of the heat, they were designed to keep sunlight out.

THE PALACE
The palace and the great temples were the centre of Egyptian life. The king's palace was also the heart of the government.

A GREAT CITY
Today, little remains of the cities of ancient Egypt. But archaeologists have shown us how the city of Thebes looked 3,000 years ago.

LIFE AT THE TOP
Houses had flat roofs and in the evening people often gathered there, as it was cooler.

LOOK OUT FOR THESE

■ **COLUMNS**
In large buildings, such as temples, the roof was supported by columns. The top of a column, called the capital, was often carved in the shape of palm leaves.

■ **CARRYING CHAIR**
The king and other important people travelled on land in a chair carried on men's shoulders, like the sedan chairs.

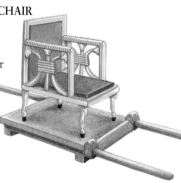

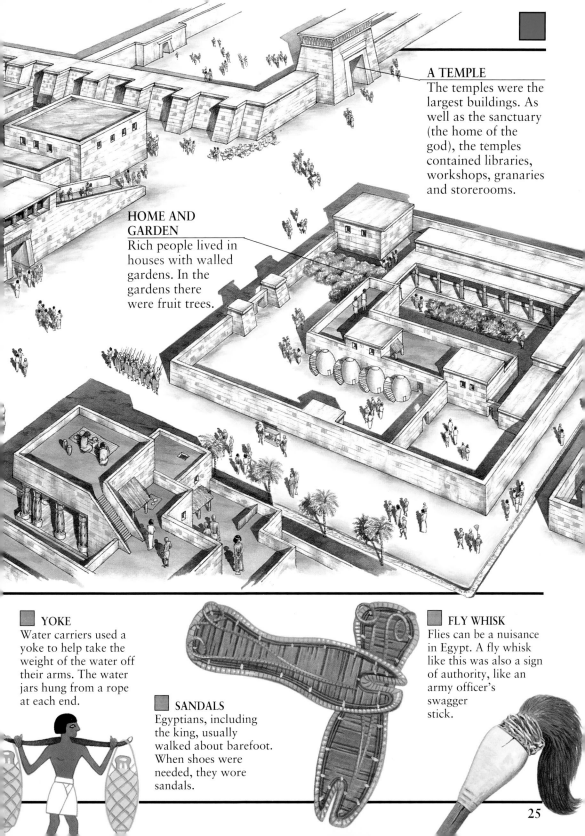

A TEMPLE
The temples were the largest buildings. As well as the sanctuary (the home of the god), the temples contained libraries, workshops, granaries and storerooms.

HOME AND GARDEN
Rich people lived in houses with walled gardens. In the gardens there were fruit trees.

YOKE
Water carriers used a yoke to help take the weight of the water off their arms. The water jars hung from a rope at each end.

SANDALS
Egyptians, including the king, usually walked about barefoot. When shoes were needed, they wore sandals.

FLY WHISK
Flies can be a nuisance in Egypt. A fly whisk like this was also a sign of authority, like an army officer's swagger stick.

25

SCULPTURE AND PAINTING

Painters and sculptors were craftsmen, like carpenters or stonemasons. Most Egyptian art that we see in museums or books comes from tombs. Painters decorated tombs with scenes from the life of the dead person. From these we can learn much about ancient Egypt.

Sculptors made figures from bronze, wood and other materials, but especially stone. They had no iron tools, only copper or bronze, but they could still shape very hard or brittle stone.

GRID
Painters in the royal tombs worked in teams and followed strict rules. They began by marking a grid pattern.

PAINTED POTTERY
The Egyptians did not often paint pottery, but they practised on broken bits, and sometimes made quick sketches.

LOOK OUT FOR THESE

SCULPTOR'S CHISEL
Sculptors shaped a stone by chipping away with a chisel and mallet. This kind of mallet is still used today.

BRUSHES
This brush is made from reeds with their ends split. Thinner brushes were used for detailed work.

PAINTER'S PALETTE
Colours were ground on a palette and mixed with water. They came from minerals, like red ochre. Black came from soot.

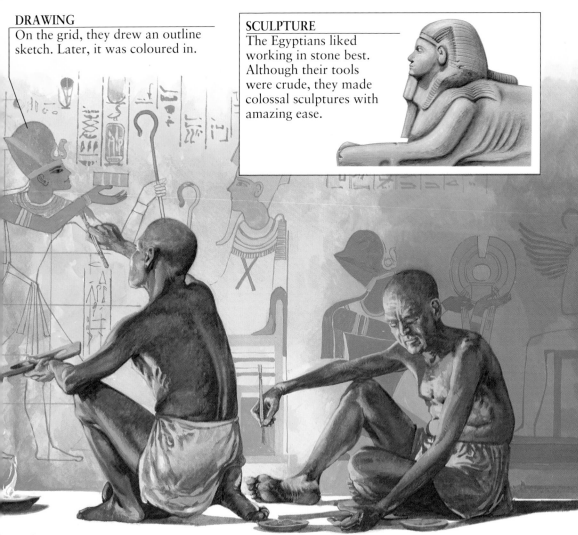

DRAWING

On the grid, they drew an outline sketch. Later, it was coloured in.

SCULPTURE

The Egyptians liked working in stone best. Although their tools were crude, they made colossal sculptures with amazing ease.

■ WOODEN FIGURE

Besides stone, smaller human figures were carved from wood. This one is a chief priest of the Old Kingdom. Small figures called ushabtis were put in important tombs. They were supposed to do any hard work for the dead person.

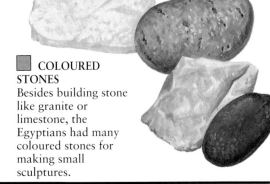

■ COLOURED STONES

Besides building stone like granite or limestone, the Egyptians had many coloured stones for making small sculptures.

CRAFTSMEN

The Egyptians were a practical people, for whom common sense and experience were important. Egyptian craftsmen were highly skilled. They learned their trade from their fathers and, in turn, taught their sons.

It is hard to understand how they made such wonderful objects with such simple tools. How could they shape and polish hard stone without iron chisels or files? If you examine their finest jewellery or furniture, you will see that it cannot be made better today.

POTTERY
Pots of many shapes and sizes were made from local clay. It was shaped by hand, in a mould made of stiff sand, given a glaze and hardened in fire.

SANDALS
The shoemaker's trade was simple, because the only shoes people wore were sandals, made of leather or papyrus reed. Usually they went barefoot.

WOOD CARVING
This man is making a wooden animal. Most woodworking tools, such as saws and chisels, have not changed much since.

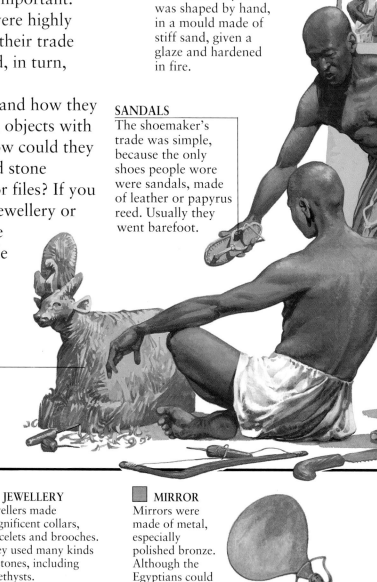

LOOK OUT FOR THESE

JEWELLERY
Jewellers made magnificent collars, bracelets and brooches. They used many kinds of stones, including amethysts.

MIRROR
Mirrors were made of metal, especially polished bronze. Although the Egyptians could make glass, they could not make it pure and true enough for mirrors.

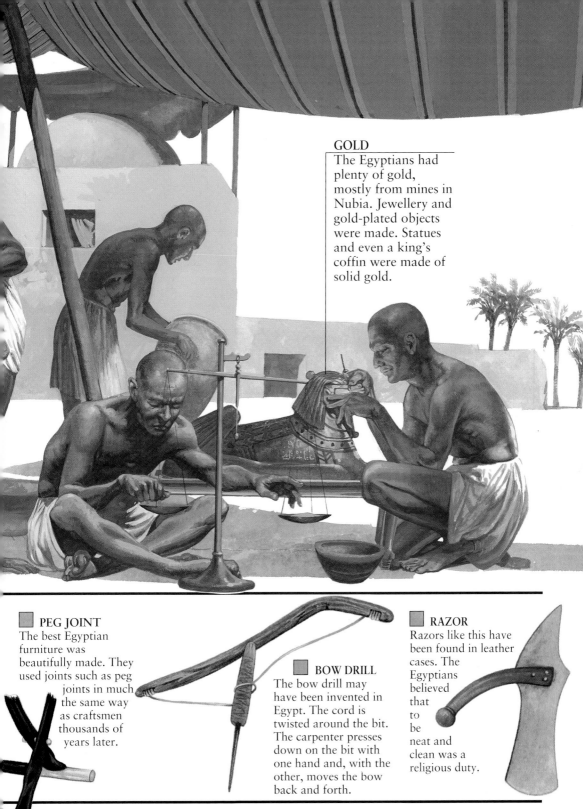

GOLD

The Egyptians had plenty of gold, mostly from mines in Nubia. Jewellery and gold-plated objects were made. Statues and even a king's coffin were made of solid gold.

■ PEG JOINT

The best Egyptian furniture was beautifully made. They used joints such as peg joints in much the same way as craftsmen thousands of years later.

■ BOW DRILL

The bow drill may have been invented in Egypt. The cord is twisted around the bit. The carpenter presses down on the bit with one hand and, with the other, moves the bow back and forth.

■ RAZOR

Razors like this have been found in leather cases. The Egyptians believed that to be neat and clean was a religious duty.

WRITING

The Egyptians invented a form of writing called hieroglyphic. Hieroglyphs are little pictures. Some stand for an object. For example, a picture of a cow means 'cow'. But they also stand for sounds. In English, you could use the sign of a cow to write the first half of the word 'cow-ard'. The same sign would stand for different words that sound alike, such as 'bow' and 'bough'. People wrote with a reed pen, or fine brush, and ink.

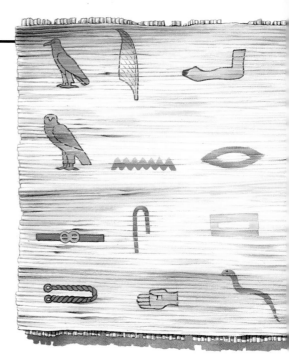

GROUP SIGNS

To write using only single letter sounds would take a very long time. Group signs made it shorter. They stood for sounds which, in English, would be made up of several different letters.

 **LOOK OUT FOR THESE**

SCRIBE'S BOX
This box has a hole for a cake of ink, and pens. Scribes were the royal officials and record keepers.

DEMOTIC
Demotic (people's writing) was a shorthand version of hieratic. It was not used until the end of the New Kingdom.

HIERATIC
As it took a long time to write hieroglyphs, scribes used a simpler form of the written language, called hieratic.

CUBIT
The cubit was based on the distance between middle finger and elbow, and was taken as 52.5cm.

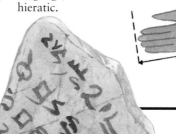

THE CALENDAR

By noting the movements of the Sun, Moon and stars, the Egyptians worked out their calendar. For example, the New Year began when Sirius, the dog star, appeared, which happened just before the Nile flooded. The year had 365 days, divided into three seasons of four months.

LETTER SIGNS

These signs stood for single sounds, like the letters of the alphabet. Vowels were left out.

SENSE SIGNS

These signs are a guide to the meaning of a word. For example, a pair of legs walking meant 'movement'.

MEASUREMENTS

This measuring rod, or ruler, measures one cubit. It was divided into seven 'hands'.

NUMBERS

These are the signs for numbers. There was no sign for 0, nor for the numbers 2-9. To write the number 435, a scribe wrote four '100' signs, three 'ten' signs and five 'one' signs. Multiplying and dividing were very complicated!

CHILDREN AND EDUCATION

Only the children of well-off people went to school. Children learned about life and religion at home. Sons of craftsmen learned their father's trade. Peasants never learned to read or write. The sons of the rich attended school in the temple. Lessons were hard. Hundreds of hieroglyphs had to be learned. Maths was also complicated.

Some children had a private tutor, and the sons of scribes had special schools until the age of 12, when they went to work. Scribes were the managers and office workers of Egypt. They also acted as tutors.

GEOMETRY
People who built pyramids had to know some geometry. They could work out areas and volumes.

EXERCISE BOOKS
Children used valuable papyrus paper only for their best work. For rough work, they wrote on stone or on a wooden board.

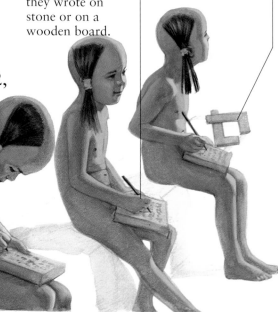

HAIRSTYLE
Young children wore their hair in a single tress, which fell to the side of the head.

LOOK OUT FOR THESE

BALL
Balls were made of wood or leather stuffed with feathers. In one game, you had to catch the ball while sitting on your partner's shoulders.

PEN AND INK
Simple pens were made of reed, sharpened to a point. Ink came in solid lumps and was mixed with water in an inkwell.

MOVING TOY
Clever toys have been found in tombs. This one opens and shuts its mouth as it is pulled along. Some girls had dolls which could be dressed.

THROWING STICK
Boys had small throwing sticks, like the bigger ones used by their fathers to hunt game. They were shaped like a boomerang.

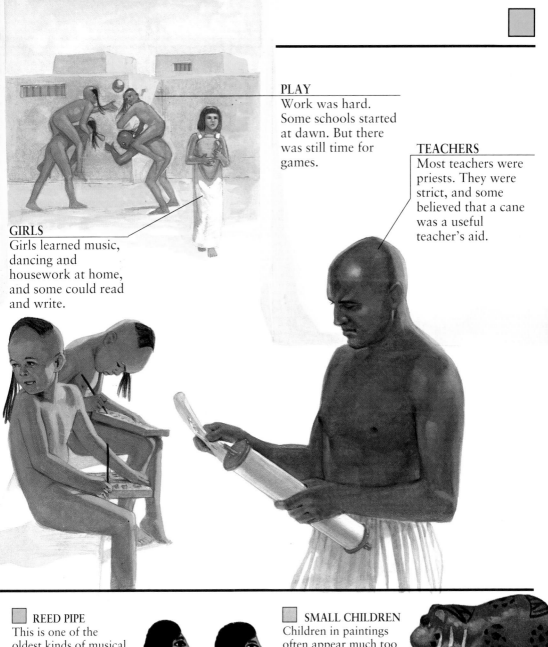

PLAY
Work was hard. Some schools started at dawn. But there was still time for games.

TEACHERS
Most teachers were priests. They were strict, and some believed that a cane was a useful teacher's aid.

GIRLS
Girls learned music, dancing and housework at home, and some could read and write.

REED PIPE
This is one of the oldest kinds of musical instrument. Often called a flute, it is really more like the recorder played today.

SMALL CHILDREN
Children in paintings often appear much too small compared with adults. The size was not meant to be realistic. It was an indication of a person's importance.

HIPPOPOTAMUS
Many small pottery hippos were made. Hippos were bad animals, linked with the evil god Seth, but these comic models were probably toys.

FARMERS

The most important business in Egypt was farming. Most of the people were peasants, who worked all day in fields and barns.

The main food crops were wheat and barley, but many vegetables and some fruits were grown in gardens. Seed was sown after the flood waters had gone down. Crops had to be watered with the help of canals and ditches. Cattle, sheep and goats gave meat and milk. Some people kept ducks and pigeons, but chickens were unknown.

During the flood season, when no farming could be done, peasants did building work on temples and palaces.

HARVEST

When the main crops were ready, nearly everyone – men and women, even priests – helped with the harvest.

TAXES

Farmers paid part of their crop as taxes. Scribes kept careful records of the amounts.

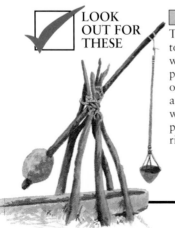

LOOK OUT FOR THESE

SHADUF

The shaduf was used to raise water. A pole was balanced on a pivot, with a weight at one end and a bucket at the other. The weight made it easy to pull up water from a river or a well.

SICKLE

Men cut the stalks of corn with a sickle. Modern sickles are much the same shape, but this one is wooden and has teeth of flint. It was used like a saw.

FLAX

Flax is an annual plant with blue flowers. Fibres from the stem are used to make linen thread. Nearly all clothes were linen.

MUSIC
Musicians played while work went on in the fields. At seed time, magic spells were chanted to make the crops grow.

WINNOWING
Women scooped the grain up with wooden trays, letting the chaff blow away while the heavier grain fell to the ground.

CATTLE
Young boys helped to look after the livestock. A man's wealth could be judged by the cattle he owned. Farmers also owned sheep, goats and donkeys.

■ **WINE**
Grapes were grown to eat and to make into wine, which was stored in stone jars. The name of the vineyard and the vintage was sometimes written on the jar, as on a modern bottle of wine. This is a fine jug of silver and gold that may have been used at important celebrations.

■ **PLOUGH**
The plough was drawn by oxen and guided by a ploughman. The main part was a heavy, sharpened stake, which only scratched up the soil. The ground was ploughed after the seed had been scattered over it, to help cover the seed.

TRADE AND SHIPS

The Egyptians did not use money. They paid taxes in the form of goods. All trade was barter, which means swapping one kind of goods for another. Wood from the Lebanon was paid for in corn and wine, for instance.

Boats of all kinds crowded the Nile. People crossed the river by ferry, while barges carried heavy cargoes. Stone for the pyramids went on giant rafts, which could carry 500 tonnes. Boats going north were helped by the current. Going south, they usually had the wind behind them.

MERCHANT SHIP
Small boats were made of bundles of reeds tied together. Larger ships were built of wood. This one sailed through the dangerous Red Sea.

GOODS FROM THE DESERT
Expeditions to the Eastern Desert brought copper, tin and other minerals from the mines. Other routes led to oases in the west.

LOOK OUT FOR THESE

WEIGHTS
The metal weight called a deben was about 90gm. It also measured value: a goat might be worth 1 deben. The value varied according to the metal (gold or copper) it was made from. A kité was one-tenth of a deben.

SCALES
These modern balance scales work in the same way as Egyptian ones. Accurate scales were needed to measure valuable things like gold.

CEDAR
Few trees grew in Egypt, but cedar wood was imported from Byblos in the Lebanon, where descendants of the famous Cedars of Lebanon still grow.

CARGO

Ships had no deck, except for short sections at each end, and the crew stowed cargo in the open hold. The ship had oars and one large sail.

THE LAND OF PUNT

Ships that sailed to Punt were carried across the desert in pieces and built on the shore of the Red Sea. Punt was probably in East Africa, but nobody knows exactly where.

MYRRH

Myrrh trees are spiny shrubs. The inner bark produces sweet-smelling gum, which was used as incense. The shrubs did not grow in Egypt, but traders brought them from Punt.

JEWEL STONES

Coloured stones and gems for jewellery came from desert mines. Sinai produced turquoise. The Eastern Desert contained emeralds.

FAMILY LIFE

An important man might have many wives (the king had hundreds). The chief wife was her husband's partner. She ran the house, and she owned the household goods. She did not have to do much housework, because she had servants, who also helped with her clothes and make-up, and arranged her hair.

Among rich people, marriages were arranged. The king married foreign princesses for political reasons. Other marriages were based on love and respect. Husband and wife were often painted with arms around each other. Families were large, with five or six children.

SERVANTS
A rich Egyptian family had servants to work for them.

CHILDREN
The Egyptians enjoyed family life, and liked children. Parents expected their children to respect them and obey them.

LOOK OUT FOR THESE

MAKE-UP
Kohl, in the form of a paste made from powder, was kept in jars. Cosmetics were mixed with metal spatulas. The mirror is made of polished bronze.

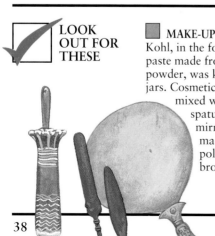

HEAD REST
Everyone had one of these. It was made to measure, and if you slept on your side, it kept your head level. It was cooler than a cushion, but not very comfortable. People may have put a cushion on top.

A HOMELY GOD

Gods lived in ordinary houses as well as temples. Bes was a favourite during the New Kingdom.

BEAUTY TREATMENT

Here a woman is making herself beautiful. After a thorough wash, she puts on her jewellery and does her hair. Then she makes up her face. Most important are the eyes. She gives them a dark outline with kohl.

PETS

The Egyptians were fond of animals. They kept birds and monkeys, as well as cats and dogs.

PAW FOOT

The legs of furniture often ended in feet shaped like a lion's paws.

BROOM

This type of broom is made of reeds, straw or twigs tied to a wooden handle. You might have one like it in your home.

BASTET

The goddess Bastet began as a lion but by the time of the New Kingdom, she had become a cat. All cats were sacred to her, and hundreds of mummified cats have been found. They were buried in the grounds of Bastet's temple in the Delta.

FOOD AND DRINK

The peasants ate mostly bread, which was baked at home every day, and vegetables such as beans, lentils, onions, leeks and turnips. Richer people ate a lot of meat and game, especially birds, which they trapped in the Delta. Although the Nile was full of fish, people did not eat fish if they could get meat. Salads of lettuce and cucumber were popular. Sweet dishes were made with honey.

People ate with their fingers – no forks or spoons were provided. The food was served in dishes and jars of pottery.

MAKING BEER
Beer was the main drink. It was made from under-cooked barley loaves, which were soaked and mashed up by trampling. The mash was left to ferment, then strained into jars.

MAKING BREAD
Women ground wheat and barley into flour and baked many kinds of loaves and cakes in a clay oven.

LOOK OUT FOR THESE

NETS
Ropes and nets were woven from twine made from the fibres of reeds. Fishermen made different kinds of net, such as seine nets or clap nets, which are still used in many parts of the world today. Nets were also used to trap wildfowl in the marshes.

FRUIT
The Egyptians had fewer fruits than we enjoy today. Grapes, figs and dates grew in vineyards and gardens.

FISHING

People were particular about which fish they ate. It was mostly eaten by the poor. The main fishing fleets were in the Delta and the Faiyum lake. Here, a net is stretched between two boats to catch fish.

MAKING WINE

Grapes were crushed by trampling, and the juice was drained off and stored in pottery jars, to ferment into wine.

BEEF

Meat was very popular, with roast beef being the favourite of the rich. But the poor had to make do with pork.

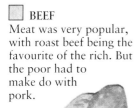

BEER STRAINER

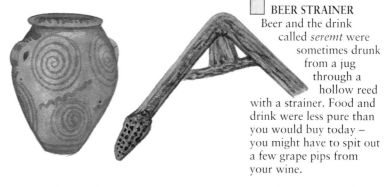

Beer and the drink called *seremt* were sometimes drunk from a jug through a hollow reed with a strainer. Food and drink were less pure than you would buy today – you might have to spit out a few grape pips from your wine.

GAMES AND HUNTING

Many kinds of everyday objects have been found in Egyptian tombs. Among them are board games and toys. Girls played with dolls, and boys had toy hunting weapons. Pictures in the tombs show children playing games like hopscotch and leapfrog, and young men wrestling. Children played ball games too.

Adults also played games, but the main sport for men was hunting. In the New Kingdom they hunted lions from a chariot, using a bow and arrow.

HUNTING FISH

The picture below illustrates how an Egyptian would sometimes spear fish from his papyrus boat.

HIPPO HUNT

Hippos were linked with the evil god Seth. Brave men hunted them. Trying to spear an angry hippo while standing on a small boat in the river was very dangerous, and hunting parties were made up of many boats. Hippos were the largest animals hunted.

LOOK OUT FOR THESE

HUNTING DOGS

People kept several kinds of dogs. Some pet dogs were buried close to their owners. This is the kind of dog kept for hunting. With its slim body and long legs, it was a fast runner. It was probably the ancestor of the greyhound.

SISTRUM

The sistrum was a kind of rattle. It was a symbol of the goddess Hathor, who loved music.

GAME PIECE

This stone disc belonged to some kind of game. Perhaps it was used in a gambling game, like the chips in a casino today.

 ORYX
The oryx is a type of large antelope, which the Egyptians hunted in the desert.

FISH HOOK
Fish hooks have hardly changed since ancient times. Egyptians made hooks of copper or bronze. They also caught fish in nets.

SENET
Board games were popular. Senet was something like snakes and ladders. If you landed on a 'good' square, you could go forward. A 'bad' square held you back.

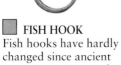

HARPOON
Harpoons had a point, a barb (to stop them coming out), and a hook for attaching a rope.

GLOSSARY

Words in SMALL CAPITAL letters indicate a cross-reference.

Abu Simbel A place in UPPER EGYPT where two temples were moved to a new site to escape flooding in 1967.

Alexander the Great A Greek king who conquered Egypt and other lands in the 4th century BC.

amulet A magic charm.

Amun Amun became the chief god of the New Kingdom and was called 'king of the gods'.

Ankh A symbol meaning 'life'. It was carried by gods and kings.

Assyria A kingdom in Mesopotamia, which conquered Egypt in the 7th century BC.

Aswan A town near the first cataract (falls), of the Nile. It marked the boundary between Egypt and Nubia.

barter Trade in which one kind of goods is exchanged for another, not paid for in money.

Byblos A port in LEBANON which was an important place for trade.

canopic jars Jars in which the organs of a dead person were placed when the body was mummified.

cedar A tree which gave good timber for building. Forests of cedars grew in LEBANON.

deben A metal ring used for measuring weight. One deben was about 90gm.

Delta The region where the river Nile splits up into several channels before reaching the Mediterranean Sea.

demotic A way of writing, quicker than HIERATIC, invented in the Late Period.

dynasty Rulers belonging to one royal 'house' or family.

Faiyum A large lake west of the Nile.

Giza A place near the modern capital of Egypt, Cairo, where the largest pyramids can be seen.

Hatshepsut A queen of the the 18th Dynasty, who ruled as pharaoh.

henna A red or orange dye made from the twigs and leaves of certain shrubs.

hieratic A simpler way of writing HIEROGLYPHS.

hieroglyphs The signs or little pictures, standing for sounds, which made up Egyptian writing.

Horus The god Horus was often shown as a hawk. He was the god most closely linked with the living pharaoh.

Hyskos A race of 'foreigners', who ruled Egypt during the Second Intermediate Period.

incense The resin or gum of certain trees, which gives off a sweet smell when burned.

Karnak A place near Thebes where some of the greatest temples of the New Kingdom were built.

Lebanon A country on the eastern Mediterranean, where Egypt traded for timber and other goods.

lotus A type of water lily. It was a symbol of UPPER EGYPT.

Lower Egypt The part of the country between MEMPHIS and the Mediterranean Sea.

magic eye The magic eye, or Eye of Horus, is a sign of the Sun or Moon. It was a good-luck sign and protected against evil spells.

malachite An ore of copper, green in colour.

Memphis The capital of the Old Kingdom. It marked the boundary between UPPER and LOWER EGYPT.

mummy A dead body which has been preserved to prevent it rotting.

myrrh Gum from the myrrh tree, which was used as incense and in mummification.

Nefertiti Wife of the pharaoh Akhenaten (18th Dynasty), who was famous for her beauty.

obelisk A monument in the form of a tall pointed pillar with flat sides.

Osiris A god who looked after the growth of plants and has a green skin. He was both husband and brother of Isis.

papyrus A reed, which grows beside the Nile, from which paper was made. It was a symbol of LOWER EGYPT.

pharaoh The king who was not only the ruler of Egypt but also a god. As ruler, he was linked with the royal god HORUS. Sometimes he is seen as the sun god, Ra. After his death, he became joined with OSIRIS.

Punt An unknown land in East Africa or south Arabia, where Egyptians traded.

pylon A huge gateway to a temple.

pyramid A tomb built of stone, square at the bottom with sides sloping up to a point.

scribe A trained clerk or record keeper.

scroll Sheets of PAPYRUS joined together and rolled up. Scrolls came before books.

senet A board game played with counters.

shaduf A machine for raising water from a well or ditch.

Sinai The desert of north-east Egypt, above the Red Sea.

sistrum A type of rattle. It was a symbol of the goddess Hathor.

sphinx A figure with a human head and lion's body.

Thebes The capital of Egypt during the New Kingdom.

Tutankamun A king of the 18th Dynasty whose tomb was discovered, undamaged, in 1922.

Upper Egypt The southern part of the country, between MEMPHIS and ASWAN.

ushabtis Small figures, like dolls, placed in tombs to act as servants in the next life.

vizier The most powerful man after the PHARAOH was the vizier, or chief minister.

INDEX

Abu Simbel 17
Alexander the Great 18
amulets 23
Amun 20
Ankh 21
Anubis 8, 22
Assyrians 18
Aswan dam 16

ball games 32, 42
Bastet 39
battle axe 18
beauty 39
beer 40, 41
Bes 39
board games 42, 43
bow and arrows 19, 42
bow drill 29
bread 40
brushes 26
burial chamber 12, 22

calendar 31
canopic jars 22
carrying chair 24
cataracts 9
cats 39
cattle 34, 35
Cedars of Lebanon 36–37
chariot 42
Cheops 12
children 32–33, 38
chisel 26
cities 24–25
clothes 38
coffin 11, 22–23
coloured stones 27
columns 24
craftsmen 28-29
cubit 30

dagger 18
dancers 14
dates 9
deben 36
demotic 30
drawing 27
drink 15, 40–41
dynasties 11

Early Period 11
Eastern Desert 36, 37
education 32-33
Egyptian Empire 19
exercise books 32

Faiyum lake 14, 41
false beard 16
family life 38–39
farming 34–35
fish 40, 41, 43
flail 16
flax 34
fly whisk 25
food 15, 40–41
food crops 34
fruit 34, 40
funeral boat 10
furniture 29, 39

games 42–43
gardens 25
geometry 32
Giza 10, 12
goats 34, 35
goddesses 8, 20–21
gods 8, 16, 20–21, 39
gold 29
grapes 35, 41
group signs 30

hairstyle 32
harpoon 43
harvest 34
Hathor 21, 42
head rest 38
heaven 22
hieratic 30
hieroglyphic 30–31, 32
hippo hunt 42–43
Hittites 18
Horus 16, 17, 21
houses 24–25
hunting 42–43
Hyskos 18, 19

incense 23, 37
Isis 20

jewellery 28, 29, 37
Karnak 24
King Narmer 11
kohl 38, 39

language 14
leather bag 13
letter signs 30–31
loom 15
Luxor 24

magic eye 21
maidservants 15

make-up 38, 39
mallet 26
marriage 38
measurements 13, 31
meat 40
medals 19
memorial 11
Memphis 24
merchant ship 36-37
Mesopotamia 18
Middle Kingdom 11,
    14–15
minerals 36
mirrors 28
model boat 14
mummification 11,
    22–23
music 14, 35
myrrh 37

natron 22
Nefertiti 8
nets 40, 41
New Kingdom 11,
    18–19
Next World 22–23
Nile Delta 8, 40, 41, 42
Nile 8–9, 10
Nubia 14, 15, 18, 29
numbers 31

oases 8, 36
obelisk 14
offerings 21
Old Kingdom 11
oryx 43
Osiris 16, 20
ostrich fan 16

painting 26–27
palace 24
papyrus 9, 32
peg joint 29
pen and ink 32
Persians 18
pets 39
pharaohs 10, 16–17
play 33
plough 35
pottery 28, 33
priests 20–21, 22–23, 33
prisoners of war 18
Punt 37
pyramids 10, 12–13

Ra 16
Ramesses II 16

razor 29
Red Sea 36, 37
reed pipe 33
religion 20–21
royal funeral 10–11
royal headdress 17
royal crowns 11

sandals 25, 28
Scales of Anubis 23
school 32
scribes 15, 30, 32
scribe's box 30
sculpture 9, 26–27
Senet 43
sense signs 31
seremt 41
servants 38
Seth 33, 42
Seti I 22
shaduf 34
sheep 34, 35
ships 36–37
shrine 21
sickle 34
Sinai 14, 37
sistrum 42
spear 18
sphinx 10
step pyramid 13
stonemasons 12, 26

taxes 34
teachers 33
temples 20–21, 25
Thebes 24
throwing stick 32
tomb 22
topknots 14
towns 9, 24–25
toys 32
trade 36–37
Tutankamun 18

ushabtis 27

vegetables 34, 40
vizier 17

Wadjit 20
weapons 18–19
weaving 15
weights 36
wildfowl 42
wine 35, 41
writing 30–31